Sight

Text: Andreu Llamas
Illustrations: Francisco Arredondo

La vista © Copyright EDICIONES ESTE, S. A., 1995,
Barcelona, Spain

Sight Copyright © 1996 by Chelsea House Publishers, a
division of Main Line Book Co. All rights reserved.

1 3 5 7 9 8 6 4 2

Library of Congress Cataloging-in-Publication Data

Llamas, Andreu.
  [Vista. English]
    Sight / Andreu Llamas ; illustrations, Francisco Arredondo.
      p. cm. — (The Five senses of the animal world)
    Includes index.
    ISBN 0-7910-3491-7. — ISBN 0-7910-3496-8 (pbk.)
    1. Vision—Juvenile literature. 2. Physiology, Comparative—
  Juvenile literature. [1. Vision. 3. Eye. 4. Senses and sensation.]
  I. Arredondo, Francisco, ill. II. Title. III. Series.
  QP.7.L771513   1996   95-10514
  591.1'823—dc20   CIP
                                             AC

Contents

Sight

CHELSEA HOUSE PUBLISHERS
New York • Philadelphia

How Does the Eye Work?

Sight is a very important sense. It gives us an abundance of information about the outside world and helps direct our movements.

Sight depends on our eyes, which are spherical organs with light sensitive cells. In vertebrates, the walls of the eye are made up of three layered membranes: the sclera, the choroid, and the retina. The retina holds the light sensitive cells: the cones and the sticks. The sticks are far greater in number than the cones and are very sensitive to light, and it is because of them that we can see when there is little light. Conversely, the cones only work when there is adequate light. The cones give the impression of color while the sticks give images in black and white.

The shape, size, and position of the two eyes also greatly affect the images animals receive; for instance, the bigger the eyes, the more light they can take in. This is why night hunters have large eyes.

Pigeon
1,300 feet

Deer
1,640 feet

Rabbit
985 feet

Mouse
245 feet

The lynx, which has very good sight, sees its favorite prey at these distances.

At right, a diagram of the human eye shows how the eye sees. The image, in this case of a tree, is inverted on the retina. The image is transmitted along the optic nerve to the brain, where it is interpreted correctly.

VISUAL INFORMATION THAT IS TRANSMITTED TO THE BRAIN

IMAGE ON THE RETINA

OPTIC NERVE

MUSCLES MOVING THE EYE

966423

Seeing Colors

How do animals see colors? When two animals look at the same object, do they see the same thing?

Each animal sees things in its own way. One reason for this is that each species has different amounts and proportions of *photosensitive* cells.

Scientists believe that the only mammals that have cones are humans and monkeys. Therefore, sheep, dogs, pigs, and cows cannot see colors. On the other hand, many insects, a great number of reptiles, and daytime birds see in color, though in a different way than humans do.

Birds, for instance, have a more complex system of color vision than humans. Their photosensitive cells have up to five pigments that detect far more shades of color than our sight.

The density of the photosensitive cells in the retina varies greatly between species; this is why falcons can see a 1-inch-long (2.5-centimeter-long) grasshopper from a height of 1,640 feet (500 meters), but elephants and rhinoceroses cannot recognize large objects even from a distance of 98 feet (30 meters).

Bees might not be able to see red, but they can see uitraviolet colors.

If there are no cones in the retina, an animal has a black and white image of the world, so colors are replaced by different shades of gray. It is more important for these animals, such as the zebra, to detect the movement of an approaching group of lions, for instance, than colors.

Ducks are able to see more color shades than humans. The cells in their eyes have a colored oil that acts as a filter, which additionally improves their vision of colors.

The Mysterious Compound Eye

Flies and other insects see their world through a complex *mosaic*.

Insects and crustacea can see thanks to their incredible compound eyes, which are made up of a great number of lenses called ommatidia. If you could look closely at them, you would see that each ommatidium has its own (usually hexagonal) lens on the surface of the eye, which gives insect eyes their strange *reticulate* look. Each lens composes its own part of the image and sends a signal to the brain. The overall image created in the insect's brain has a mosaic form. Can you imagine how strange the world must seem through the eyes of an insect?

The greater the number of ommatidia that makes up the eye, the clearer the image and the slighter the movements that may be detected. This is why some insects have such large eyes that they take up almost the entire head.

As you can see, the structure of an insect's eye may be very complicated. The more ommatidia there are, the better the vision. Flies, for instance, have compound eyes consisting of about 20,000 ommatidia.

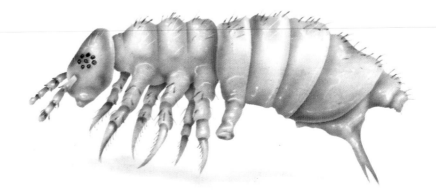

The compound eye has not yet reached perfection in some insects like this coleopteran, which has only eight ommatidia in each eye.

This fly has a very different view of the world than you have.

Compound eyes are specially designed to catch movements, as each movement stimulates several different ommatidia.

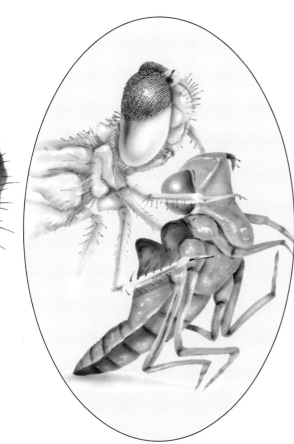

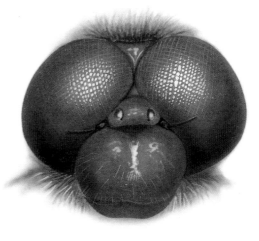

For insects that hunt in flight, like this dragonfly on the left, their sight is very important. Their eyes are made up of 30,000 ommatidia, yet their sight is 30 times worse than humans'.

Light Manufacturers

Did you know that some animals can make light with their own bodies?

Actually, there are many animals that have cells known as *photophores* and can produce light. But sometimes the animal does not produce the light it gives out, but rather has luminous bacteria on the surface of its body.

There are luminescent animals in almost all of the ocean, and scientists believe that more than 75 percent of the species that live in the ocean depths are luminescent.

Luminescence varies, and each species has distinctive colors and characteristics. Generally, all individuals of the same sex within the same species look alike.

When night falls, many insects use their luminous organs to attract the attention of possible partners. These insects are able to control the intensity of the light they give out—when a female senses the presence of a male, it accelerates its breathing rhythm to increase its light intensity.

This luminosity is a cold light with a very high luminous output. For centuries South American Indians have used lamps made with these insects.

Many fish from the abysses have developed luminous lures to attract their prey. They only have to wait for their food to come close enough.

If you could see one of these luminous traps close up, would you find it fascinating? You would see that they are made of strange, almost transparent filaments.

The luminous traps of deep-sea fish may be on different parts of the body: on the top, on the head, underneath, on the sides, or even in the mouth.

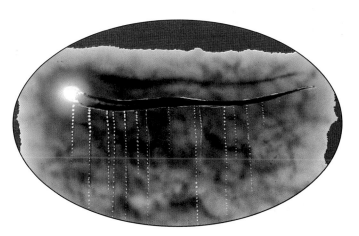

There exists a luminous worm that lives in dark caves. It makes laces of sticky droplets and lights them with the gleam from its body. When insects come close they get stuck and the worm can eat them.

The Brazilian pyrophore is an insect with two luminous spots on its body. These simulate the threatening gleam of a night predator and frighten away birds and other enemies.

LUMINOUS SPOTS

EYES

Here you can see the amazing Australian squid with its incredible, brightly-colored luminescent organs.

Seeing in the Dark

Have you ever noticed that cats' eyes shine in the dark when light hits them?

Many animals have nighttime habits and have adapted their sight to conditions of low luminosity. Generally, their eyes are quite large and have a predominance of sticks that give clear, dark images and are very sensitive to low light levels.

Actually, most mammals have more sticks than cones, because their eyes are well adapted to seeing in dim light. Some animals, like cats, have achieved an extraordinary adaptation to night vision—the lattice—a reflecting layer that many mammals have behind their retina.

Thanks to this layer of reflecting cells that act like small mirrors, there is a far greater chance of images reaching the retina. Since beams do a return journey through it, they have twice the chance. The eyes of these animals shine when they are lit in darkness.

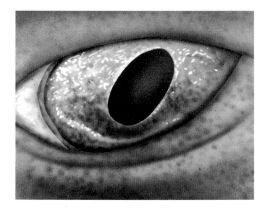

The eyes of some fish, such as this shark, also have a reflective layer behind the retina.

Felines such as these lions have a reflective layer behind the retina that greatly increases their night sight. This is why when groups of lions go out hunting at dusk, their eyes gleam threateningly in the darkness.

The eyes of felines, such as this cat, gleam at night as if they were ghost hunters.

Nocturnal birds of prey have extraordinary sight. Thanks to their sight and their hearing, they become fearful hunters when night falls.

Incredible Infrared Sight

Did you know that rattlesnakes never fail when they attack prey, even in the darkness of night?

There are two families of snakes—rattlers (including pit vipers, such as the rattlesnake) and constrictors (such as boa, python, and anaconda)—that have developed a perfect system for detecting their prey: *infrared* sight.

In darkness, the snake approaches its victims guided by the infrared beams that their bodies give out. The snake catches these beams with its thermosensitive pits that are able to detect the slightest change in temperature. These pits are very useful for hunting both during the day and at night, even in the darkness of rodents' hideouts.

Thanks to its infallible infrared sight, the pit viper detects its prey's body heat.

Here you can see how the rattlesnake uses its thermal eyes to discover the direction in which its prey is hidden.

The thermal eyes of the rattlesnake are so perfect that they can detect temperature changes of as little as 0.003 degrees Celcius.

In boas, the infrared receivers are very sensitive and can react to temperature changes in as little as 0.035 seconds.

THREE IMAGES OF A SNAKE'S WORLD

A snake's view of the world is very different from a human's, because its mind combines visual and infrared information.

COMPLETE VISUAL IMAGE AND INFRARED INFORMATION

VISUAL INFORMATION

INFRARED INFORMATION

A Bird's-Eye View

Did you know that vultures have the keenest sight of all animals?

When it gets hot, vultures glide up to over 6,560 feet (2,000 meters) on air currents, and from there they can see for many miles. No animal corpse can escape their eyes!

A vulture's sight is successful thanks to a special adaptation of its eyes; the central part of its range of vision is augmented 2.5 times, just like a *zoom*. This part of the retina has a higher concentration of light-sensitive cells, so it can catch all details.

Have you ever noticed that eyes are in a different positions in each species? Actually, most potential prey have eyes on each side of their head for a panoramic view. The further apart the eyes are, the wider the field of vision and the more difficult it is for them to be surprised by a predator. By contrast, predators always seem to have narrower vision, with their eyes facing more forward so they only see all details in the central circle (like humans).

The falcon falls upon its prey at more than 180 miles per hour (300 kilometers per hour), so it needs perfect sight in order to aim accurately.

As you can see in the picture at right, a vulture views the central part of its field of vision as though it were through a telephoto lens, so it can see all the details better.

The eyes of birds of prey, such as this partridge hunting eagle, point forward to see prey from a great height before coming down to catch them.

Seeing Underwater

Sight under the sea is very different from sight on land.

The light that enters the sea is absorbed and dispersed, so beyond about 100 feet (30 meters) below the surface everything is a dark blue color. Light disappears deeper down, and below 1,970 feet (600 meters) humans' eyes can no longer detect any light.

Nevertheless, this is not true for all the animals that live in the sea, because many have adapted their eyes to be able to see well, even at a great depth.

Most fish have their eyes far apart so their vision is monocular, which means that each eye sees different things. In other words, the left eye sees what is on the left of its body and the right eye sees what is on the right. Each eye alone watches a visual angle of some 150 degrees.

In any case, most fish sway their bodies while they are swimming, so everything can be explored at the same time.

There is a freshwater fish called anableps that spends most of its time floating on the surface of the water. It has two "split" eyes, which enable it to watch above and below the water at the same time.

Each eye of the shark has a visual angle of 150 degrees, which means it can see 300 degrees or more with both eyes together. When swimming, the swinging movement of its body allows it to see almost all around itself.

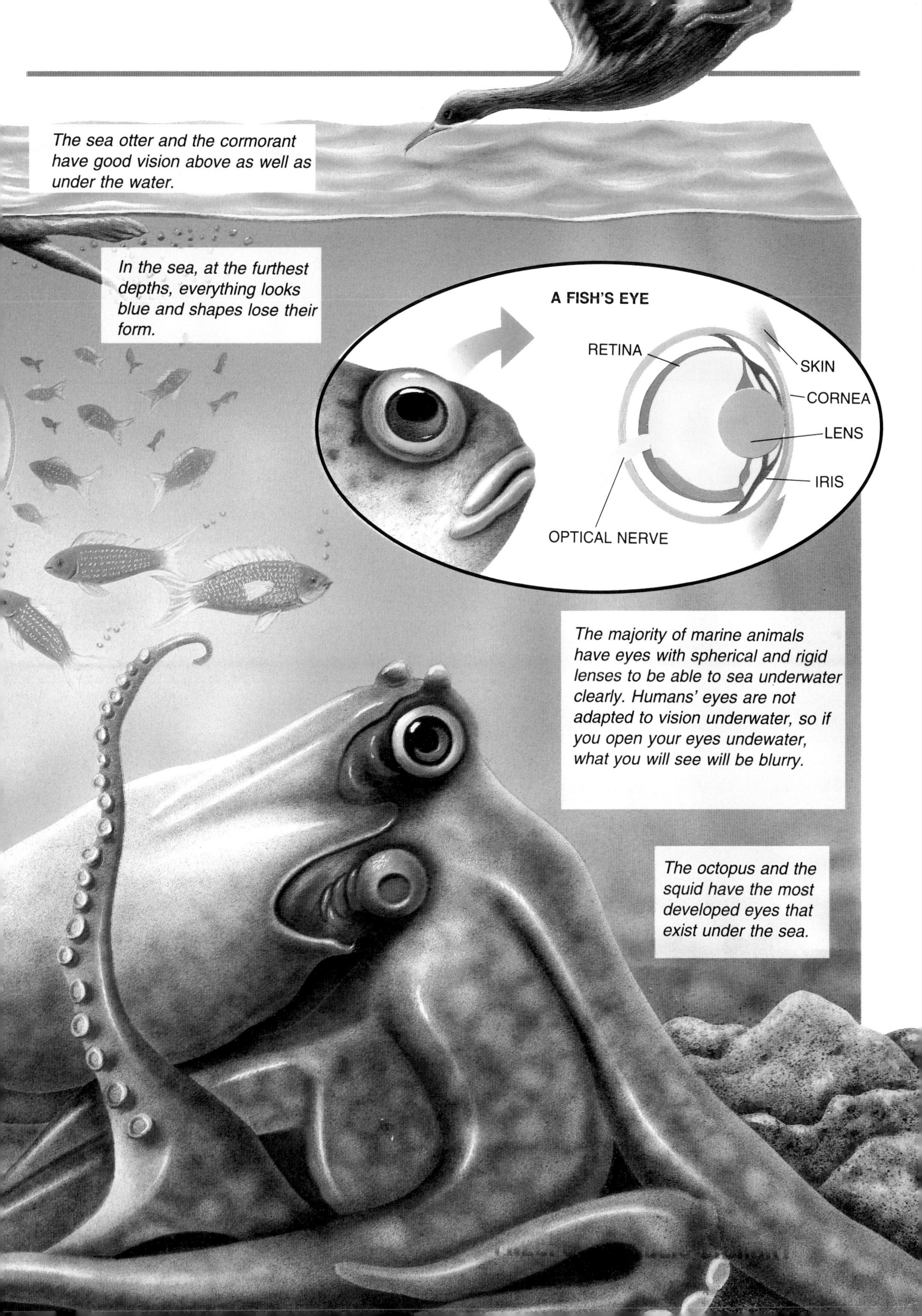

The sea otter and the cormorant have good vision above as well as under the water.

In the sea, at the furthest depths, everything looks blue and shapes lose their form.

A FISH'S EYE

RETINA

SKIN

CORNEA

LENS

IRIS

OPTICAL NERVE

The majority of marine animals have eyes with spherical and rigid lenses to be able to sea underwater clearly. Humans' eyes are not adapted to vision underwater, so if you open your eyes undewater, what you will see will be blurry.

The octopus and the squid have the most developed eyes that exist under the sea.

Through the Eyes of Amphibians

Amphibians were the first animals to develop eyelids. They were also the first to have tears.

When amphibians evolved from fish, their eyes developed new structures to function out of the water. For example, to prevent the eye from drying, most of the cells of the epidermis hardened and became rich in *keratin*.

Amphibians were also the first animals to invent mobile folds in their skin to protect their eyes—eyelids. Amphibians have three eyelids: the upper and lower are thick and are the same color as the animal and the third eyelid, which humans do not have, is thin, almost transparent, stuck to the eye, and is called the nictitating membrane.

Did you know that amphibians were the first animals to have tears? Tears have two purposes: first, the fluid spreads across the whole eye so the cells of the outer layer can stay alive to carry out their function, even out of the water; and second, tears contain a substance called lysozyme, which protects the eyes against the microorganisms that continually get under the eyelids.

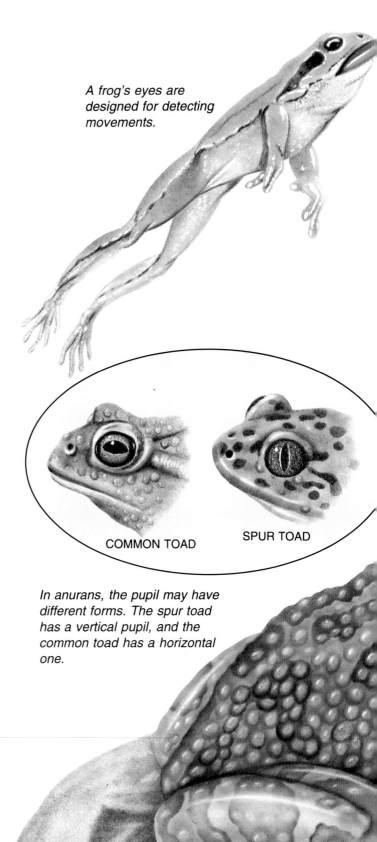

A frog's eyes are designed for detecting movements.

COMMON TOAD   SPUR TOAD

In anurans, the pupil may have different forms. The spur toad has a vertical pupil, and the common toad has a horizontal one.

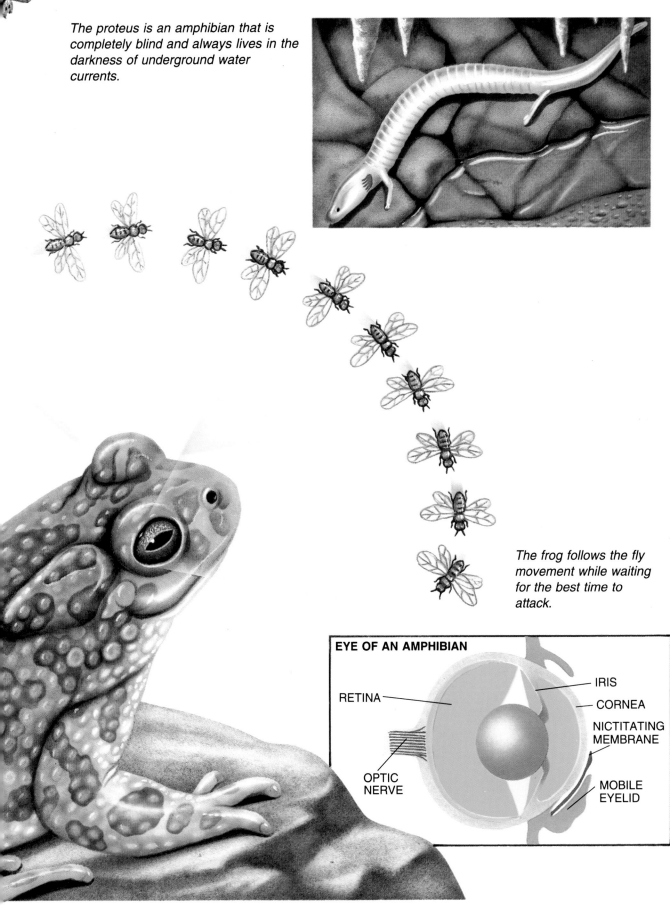

The proteus is an amphibian that is completely blind and always lives in the darkness of underground water currents.

The frog follows the fly movement while waiting for the best time to attack.

EYE OF AN AMPHIBIAN

RETINA

IRIS

CORNEA

NICTITATING MEMBRANE

OPTIC NERVE

MOBILE EYELID

Reptiles' Vision

We see the whole range of possibilities in reptile vision, from very well-sighted species to others that are practically blind.

The eyes of most reptiles are obviously better adapted to life on land than amphibians' eyes. The eyes of most reptiles, except snakes, are protected by eyelids that are far more mobile than those of amphibians, although the lower eyelid is still larger. They also have a real nictitating membrane.

Additionally, all reptiles produce tear secretion, with the exception of sphenodons, chameleons, and ophidians. Scientists agree that tortoises and lizards have color vision but doubt that crocodiles and snakes do.

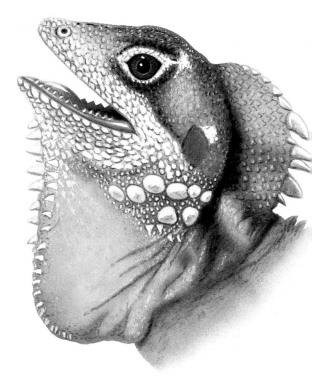

Many reptiles can see in color, so to communicate they use postures and movements that make their extraordinary color combinations stand out. Actually, color is used for distinguishing between sexes in many lizard species.

All aquatic and semiaquatic predators have eyes on top of their heads so they can see and stalk their prey while remaining hidden, almost submerged, as the picture of this terrible crocodile shows.

Snakes do not have eyelids but have eyes covered by a transparent window, a crystal lens, which gives them a glassy look. Snakes' sight varies greatly between species: there are blind snakes that can only distinguish light and darkness, and there are also daylight snakes with very keen sight.

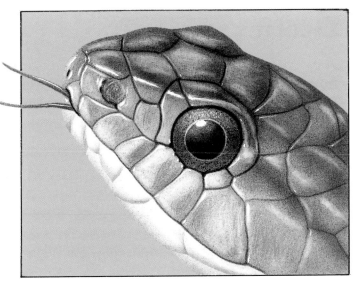

A chameleon's sight is incredible.
When it sees a prey it leaves one eye focused on it while it approaches and the other eye looks around in case some enemy lurks. To do this, its eyes can rotate and are situated on "towers."

Deceit

Sight is of extreme importance for most predators, so many of their possible victims try to deceive them in order to survive, especially if they are weak and their bodies are soft and tasty.

Animals use various color combinations to camouflage themselves. The simplest method of all is to imitate the color of the background. If the animal spends all its life on a background of the same color, the camouflage may be simple (like the white polar bear, which always lives in snow and arctic ice). On the other hand, some animals have a series of color bands or stripes crossing their bodies, because light and dark colors alternately "break up" and disguise the shape of the body. It is also important to hide certain parts of the body, such as feet, the neck, or wings, which usually attract attention and give away the prey.

There are fish, such as this sea dragon, which have developed strange forms to deceive their predators. At first glance, they look like pieces of floating seaweed.

Predators have developed systems in order to hide from their prey. For example, the tiger's stripes and the leopard's spots are perfect camouflage in their usual hunting grounds.

The squid or cuttlefish is a master of disguise. When it moves, it can change color quickly or change shape gradually, to camouflage itself against the surrounding colors.

Here is the deadly stone fish. Its camouflage is so perfect that it is very difficult to see. If an absent-minded swimmer treads on one, he is as good as dead.

Different Eye Positions

Have you ever noticed that the eyes of animals are located in very different positions?

To make full use of their sight, each species has its eyes situated in the position that is most helpful. The eyes of predators, for example, are directed forward, because what is most important for them is to see the prey that they are chasing when hunting. If you look closely, you will see that the eyes of lions, wolves, and tigers are like this.

Prey, on the other hand, have preferred to have their eyes on each side of the head, for in this way they have a greater field of vision and as a result, their forward sight is not very good. However, it is easier for them to detect when an enemy is approaching.

By contrast, there are some animals who have increased their field of vision by having their eyes located somewhat removed from their bodies, on the end of antennae or tentacles (such as snails' horns).

One special case is the fish that bury themselves in the sand so as not to be discovered by prey or predators. Their eyes stick out from their bodies and continue to look while the rest of their body is buried.

Rabbits have better sight on the sides of their bodies.

The sight of predators such as this cheetah (right) is directed forward. In this way they can concentrate better on the prey they are chasing.

The hermit crab's eyes are on the end of antennae.

The hammer fish has eyes on each side of its widened head.

Flat fish have both eyes on the same side of their bodies.

False Eyes

Some animals deceive their enemies with enormous, threatening eyes that are not real.

There is a very curious way to shake off predators, and that is to direct the enemy's attack to a place where no vital organ can be hurt.

Most predators first attack the end of the head and go for their victims' eyes. In this way they attack the place where they can do them most harm. Although the victim does not die immediately, it is more likely to be incapacitated and not be able to defend itself or escape. (A zebra can flee without a tail, but not without its head!)

Some prey have developed false eyes that cause the predator to attack the wrong place. There are many ways of deceit: the simplest consists of having a large mark similar to an eye at the back of the body. Normally, the false eye is larger than the real one and the predator prefers to attack the false one. Another technique consists of hiding the real eye and making the false eye look more real.

It looks like a snake! Here you can see how the caterpillars of the papilionaceous butterfly have two false eyes on the front of their bodies, just above the real head. When it feels threatened, the caterpillar tries to frighten its enemies by raising itself like a snake and extracting an organ from the front of its body which looks like a snake's tongue.

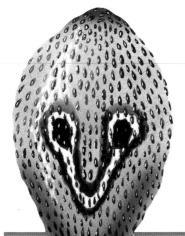

The cobra has a pair of ocular marks on its extendible neck, so no animal will dare attack it from behind as it seems to be looking directly at it.

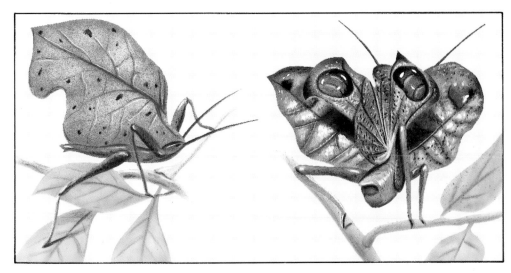

This butterfly has two large ocular spots on its wings that are usually hidden. When an enemy approaches, it opens its wings and shows these large false eyes.

The striped butterfly fish hides its eyes with a mask.

The kite fish disguises its eye among the white spots.

The pearl-colored owlet has a pair of ocular marks behind its head, so it is more difficult to know which way it is looking.

The Third Eye

Did you know that vertebrates have a third eye?

The "third eye," which is also called the pineal organ, is a structure in the brain that carries out an extremely important function in controlling biological rhythms. It is light-sensitive, but unlike the real eyes it does not contribute to sight.

So what is this third eye for? During the night, the pineal organ frees a molecule called melatonin, which acts as a detector of light intensity. It gives information on the length of the day, the night, and how long the season is. This is how the animal can live in harmony with its surroundings as it understands the rhythm of the days and seasons.

The third eye tells animals that hibernate of the right time to begin to do so and when to wake up, according to the number of hours in each day.

Additionally, reproduction in many species is seasonal, so without the information from this curious third eye, reproduction might not be successful, since the offspring would not be born at the best time of year for survival.

A mouse knows which season it is in thanks to the information it receives from its third eye.

Animals that hibernate, such as this bear, must know the right moment to go to sleep. They get this information from the pineal organ.

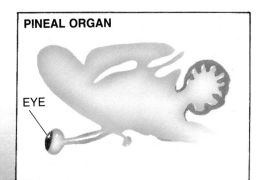

PINEAL ORGAN

EYE

Glossary

infrared lying outside the spectrum at the red end; used for thermal radiation of wavelengths longer than visible light

keratin a hard elastic protein that is present in the epidermal tissues of many parts of vertebrates' bodies, such as in feathers, hair, nails, and horns

luminescence an emission of light that occurs in low temperatures, visible in darkness

mosaic many small pieces that unite to make up one larger form

photophores light-emitting spots on various marine animals, especially deep-sea fish

photosensitive sensitive to the light; in the majority of animals the cells inside the retina are photosensitive

reticulate resembling a net or mesh

zoom to focus on a far-away object in a way that it appears much closer than it really is

Index